— VISIT —
AMERICA'S REGIONS!

Visit the PACIFIC NORTHWEST

By Kathryn Walton

Enslow PUBLISHING

Please visit our website, www.enslow.com. For a free color catalog of all our high-quality books, call toll free 1-800-398-2504 or fax 1-877-980-4454.

Library of Congress Cataloging-in-Publication Data
Names: Walton, Kathryn, 1993- author.
Title: Visit the Pacific Northwest / Kathryn Walton.
Description: Buffalo, NY : Enslow Publishing, [2024] | Series: Visit America's regions! | Includes bibliographical references and index.
Identifiers: LCCN 2023033366 (print) | LCCN 2023033367 (ebook) | ISBN 9781978537576 (library binding) | ISBN 9781978537569 (paperback) | ISBN 9781978537583 (ebook)
Subjects: LCSH: Northwest, Pacific–Description and travel–Juvenile literature.
Classification: LCC F852.3 .W36 2024 (print) | LCC F852.3 (ebook) | DDC 917.9–dc23/eng/20230803
LC record available at https://lccn.loc.gov/2023033366
LC ebook record available at https://lccn.loc.gov/2023033367

Published in 2024 by
Enslow Publishing
2544 Clinton Street
Buffalo, NY 14224

Copyright © 2024 Enslow Publishing

Portions of this work were originally authored by Kathleen Connors and published as *Let's Explore The Pacific Northwest*. All new material in this edition is authored by Kathryn Walton.

Designer: Claire Wrazin
Editor: Natalie Humphrey

Photo credits: Series art (leather spine and corners) nevodka/Shutterstock.com, (map) Karin Hildebrand Lau/Shutterstock.com, (stamped boxes) lynea/Shutterstock.com, (old paper) Siam SK/Shutterstock.com, (vintage photo frame) shyshak roman/Shutterstock.com, (visitor's guide paper background) Andrey_Kuzmin/Shutterstock.com; cover, p. 1 (main) Checubus/Shutterstock.com; cover, p. 1 (inset) Nature's Charm/Shutterstock.com; pp. 5, 21 (map) pingebat/Shutterstock.com; p. 7 Um Sixtyfour/Shutterstock.com; p. 9 Dene' Miles/Shutterstock.com; pp. 10, 20 (arrows) Elina Li/Shutterstock.com; p. 11 Marina Poushkina/Shutterstock.com, (map) Cartarium/Shutterstock.com; p. 13 melissamn/Shutterstock.com; p. 15 ARTYOORAN/Shutterstock.com; p. 17 KennStilger47/Shutterstock.com; p. 19 Dee Browning/Shutterstock.com.

All rights reserved. No part of this book may be reproduced in any form without permission in writing from the publisher, except by a reviewer.

Some of the images in this book illustrate individuals who are models. The depictions do not imply actual situations or events.

Printed in the United States of America

CPSIA compliance information: Batch #CWENS24: For further information contact Enslow Publishing at 1-800-398-2504.

CONTENTS

WELCOME TO THE PACIFIC NORTHWEST 4
GEOGRAPHY 6
READY TO ERUPT! 8
THE PUGET SOUND 10
NATIVE PEOPLES OF THE PACIFIC NORTHWEST . . 12
SEATTLE AND PORTLAND 14
WET WEATHER 16
GO GREEN 18
FAMOUS FACES 20
GLOSSARY 22
FOR MORE INFORMATION 23
INDEX 24

Words in the glossary appear in **bold** type the first time they are used in the text.

WELCOME TO THE PACIFIC NORTHWEST

The Pacific Northwest is hard to map. Depending on who you ask, the Pacific Northwest can be defined, or explained, by **geography** or weather patterns. Some also define it by culture, or the beliefs and ways of life of a group of people.

The states usually included in the Pacific Northwest are Washington and Oregon. Many people include Idaho and western Montana as well. With many national forests and a rich history, there's so much to see in the Pacific Northwest!

• VISITOR'S GUIDE •

PARTS OF BRITISH COLUMBIA IN CANADA AND NORTHERN CALIFORNIA ARE SOMETIMES INCLUDED IN THE PACIFIC NORTHWEST **REGION** TOO.

Washington, Oregon, and all or some of other states may be considered part of the Pacific Northwest.

GEOGRAPHY

Two major borders of the Pacific Northwest are the Rocky Mountains to the east and the Pacific Ocean to the west. The Rockies offer many great trails, perfect for campers looking for a hiking adventure. The Pacific Ocean is great for many kinds of fishing. Many people catch salmon, trout, and more.

A few of the largest rivers in North America are in the Pacific Northwest! The eighth-longest river in the United States, the Columbia River, cuts through the region.

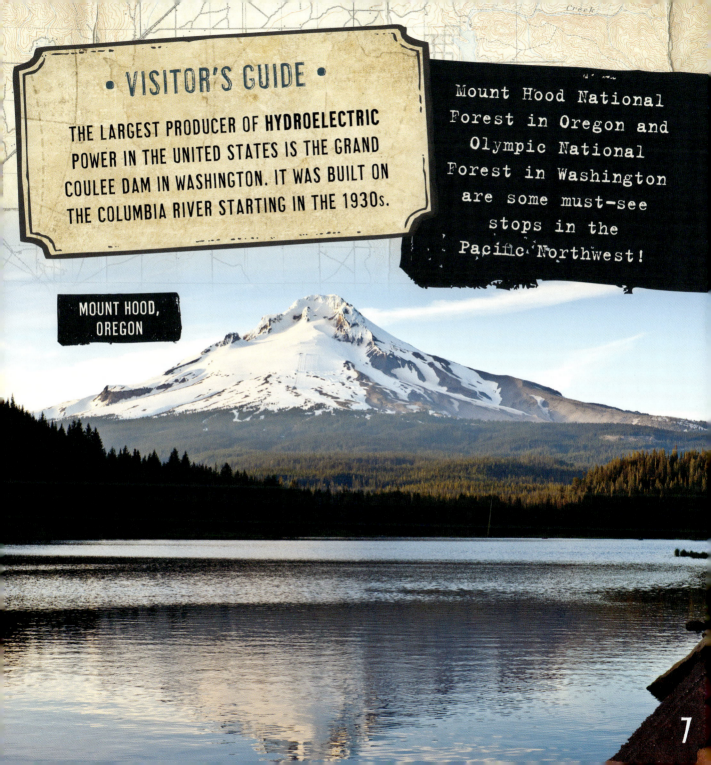

• **VISITOR'S GUIDE** •

THE LARGEST PRODUCER OF **HYDROELECTRIC** POWER IN THE UNITED STATES IS THE GRAND COULEE DAM IN WASHINGTON. IT WAS BUILT ON THE COLUMBIA RIVER STARTING IN THE 1930s.

Mount Hood National Forest in Oregon and Olympic National Forest in Washington are some must-see stops in the Pacific Northwest!

MOUNT HOOD, OREGON

READY TO ERUPT!

There are many active **volcanoes** you can visit in the Pacific Northwest. Active volcanoes are volcanoes that scientists believe could **erupt** at some time. If that were to happen, it could mean a lot of lava, or hot liquid rock, on the ground and ash in the air!

Newberry National Volcanic Monument is part of the Deschutes National Forest in central Oregon. Visitors can drive through Newberry's caldera, which is the large depression made by volcanic activity. There is volcanic rock such as basalt and obsidian everywhere!

• VISITOR'S GUIDE •

IN 1980, MOUNT ST. HELENS IN WASHINGTON ERUPTED AND DESTROYED THE FOREST AROUND IT. EVEN THOUGH MOUNT ST. HELENS COULD STILL ERUPT, PEOPLE LIKE TO CLIMB IT TODAY!

Nearly 14,000 people climb Mount St. Helens each year.

THE PUGET SOUND

The Puget Sound in Washington is a great place to visit. With many deep-water harbors, streams, and islands, this area has many lovely views! Washington's cities of Seattle and Tacoma, among others, are found on its shore. The Puget Sound area is home to about 60 percent of Washington's 7.8 million people.

The capital of Washington State, Olympia, is also on the Puget Sound. Those visiting Olympia can enjoy art, music, and theater there.

> The Puget Sound has many islands for people to visit, including Anderson Island, Bainbridge Island, Blake Island, and more!

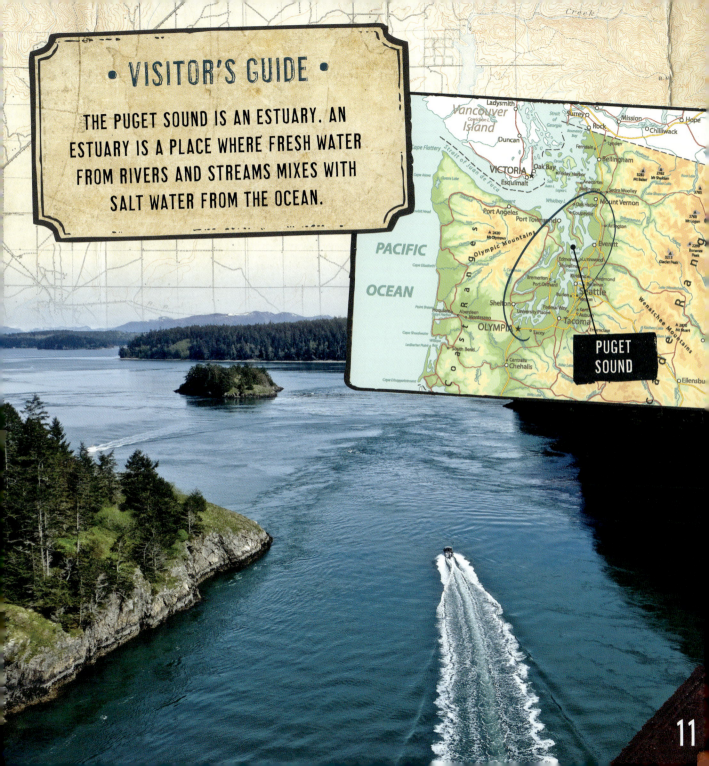

• VISITOR'S GUIDE •

THE PUGET SOUND IS AN ESTUARY. AN ESTUARY IS A PLACE WHERE FRESH WATER FROM RIVERS AND STREAMS MIXES WITH SALT WATER FROM THE OCEAN.

PUGET SOUND

NATIVE PEOPLES OF THE PACIFIC NORTHWEST

Long before European settlers came to the Pacific Northwest, Native Americans such as the Lummi and Puyallup peoples were already living there. Today, many groups keep their history alive by practicing **traditions** passed down over hundreds of years. Visitors may even be able to see some of these traditions firsthand.

Travelers in the Pacific Northwest can also visit **museums** that showcase Native American history. They can see battlefields where Native peoples fought to keep their homes safe from European settlers.

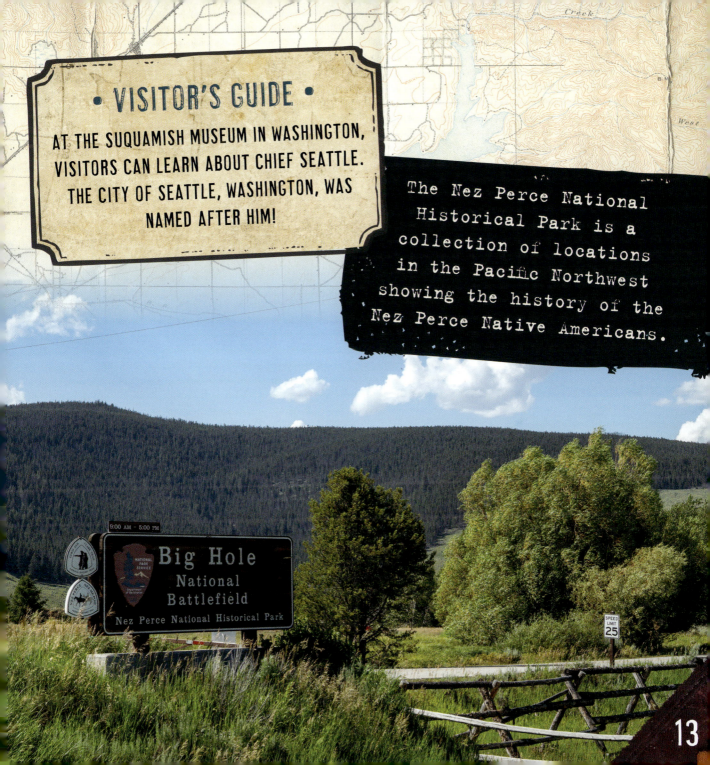

- **VISITOR'S GUIDE** -

AT THE SUQUAMISH MUSEUM IN WASHINGTON, VISITORS CAN LEARN ABOUT CHIEF SEATTLE. THE CITY OF SEATTLE, WASHINGTON, WAS NAMED AFTER HIM!

The Nez Perce National Historical Park is a collection of locations in the Pacific Northwest showing the history of the Nez Perce Native Americans.

SEATTLE AND PORTLAND

Seattle, Washington, is a great place to visit on any trip through the Pacific Northwest! Catch a Mariners baseball game or visit the displays of the interactive Museum of Pop Culture. Head underground to explore streets—now tunnels—of a Seattle area that burned down in the late 1800s. Parts of present-day Seattle are built over it!

Portland, Oregon, is another great road trip stop. The Oregon Zoo and Powell's City of Books are both must-see locations in Portland.

• VISITOR'S GUIDE •

OVER 635,000 PEOPLE LIVE IN PORTLAND, MAKING IT THE SECOND BIGGEST CITY IN THE PACIFIC NORTHWEST. THE LARGEST CITY, SEATTLE, HAS ABOUT 749,000 PEOPLE.

Mill Ends Park in Portland is the smallest park in the world!

WET WEATHER

The Pacific Northwest gets a lot of rain, so make sure to bring a raincoat if you visit! Washington's Olympic Peninsula can have 140 inches (356 cm) of **precipitation** a year. Northwest California often gets even more. The coast of Oregon is also very wet.

Temperatures range widely across the Pacific Northwest. It may be only 60°F (16°C) in the Cascade Range of mountains in July, while Spokane, Washington, can top 100°F (38°C) during summer!

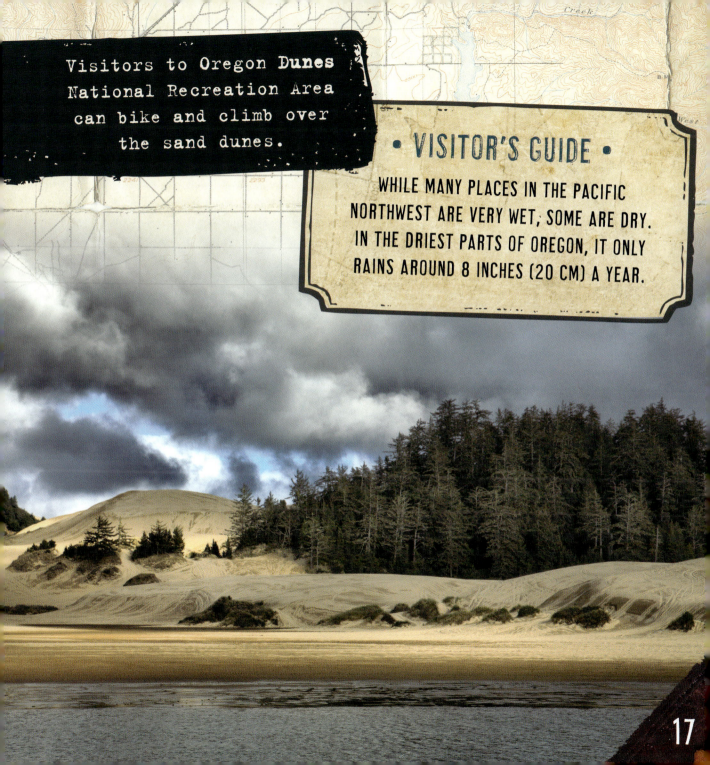

Visitors to Oregon Dunes National Recreation Area can bike and climb over the sand dunes.

• VISITOR'S GUIDE •

WHILE MANY PLACES IN THE PACIFIC NORTHWEST ARE VERY WET, SOME ARE DRY. IN THE DRIEST PARTS OF OREGON, IT ONLY RAINS AROUND 8 INCHES (20 CM) A YEAR.

GO GREEN

Many people from the Pacific Northwest are well known for **conservation**. Portland, Oregon, is regularly called one of the greenest cities in America! Seattle is right behind it.

Many groups in the Pacific Northwest, including the U.S. Forestry Service, work to save wildlife in the region. You can learn a lot about wildlife at the Pacific Northwest's many national parks! North Cascades National Park, Lewis and Clark National Park, and others are all must-see stops.

• **VISITOR'S GUIDE** •

THOUSANDS OF TREES ARE PLANTED EACH YEAR IN OREGON ALONE!

Portland is often called the No. 1 most bike-friendly city, with more than 22,000 people who bike to work.

FAMOUS FACES

The famous guitar player Jimi Hendrix and Microsoft cofounder Bill Gates were both born in Seattle, Washington. The cartoonist behind *The Simpsons* and *Disenchantment*, Matt Groening, is also from the Pacific Northwest. He was born in Portland.

The Pacific Northwest has many stops for history lovers, nature explorers, and anyone who wants to discover a new culture. You won't want to miss anything on your trip through this region!

• VISITOR'S GUIDE •

HAVE YOU EVER WANTED TO TAKE THE SAME PATH AS EARLY SETTLERS? STEP ONTO THE OREGON TRAIL! VISITORS TO THE PACIFIC NORTHWEST CAN WALK PARTS OF THIS 2,000-MILE (3,219 KM) TRAIL THAT MANY SETTLERS FOLLOWED, HOPING TO FIND A NEW HOME.

MORE THINGS TO SEE IN THE PACIFIC NORTHWEST

PIKE PLACE MARKET
This open-air market in Seattle, Washington, doesn't just have vendors throwing fish, it also has the first Starbucks coffee location!

Check out more places to stop on your trip through the Pacific Northwest!

SHOSHONE ICE CAVES
In Shoshone, Idaho, visitors can explore caves with year-round ice!

MICROSOFT VISITOR CENTER
Stop by Microsoft's Visitor Center in Redmond, Washington, and learn the history of the company and what it's planning for the future.

CRATER LAKE NATIONAL PARK
Created by a volcanic eruption over 7,700 years ago, this lake in southern Oregon is a must-see stop.

GLOSSARY

conservation: The care of the natural world.

dune: A sand hill created by wind.

erupt: To burst forth.

geography: The study of Earth and its features.

hydroelectric: Having to do with creating power by using the movement of water.

museum: A building in which things of interest are displayed.

precipitation: Rain, snow, sleet, or hail.

region: A large area of land that has features that make it different from nearby areas of land.

tradition: Custom practiced for a long time by certain cultures and people.

volcano: An opening in a planet's surface through which hot, liquid rock sometimes flows.

FOR MORE INFORMATION

Books

Perish, Patrick. *Oregon*. Minneapolis, MN: Bellwether Media, Inc., 2022.

Rathburn, Betsy. *Idaho*. Minneapolis, MN: Bellwether Media, Inc., 2022.

Websites

Britannica Kids: Oregon
www.kids.britannica.com/kids/article/Oregon/345515
Learn more about the history of Oregon.

National Geographic Kids: Native People of the American Northwest Coast
www.kids.nationalgeographic.com/history/article/native-people-of-the-american-northwest-coast
Discover more about the people who lived in the Pacific Northwest before European settlers.

Publisher's note to educators and parents: Our editors have carefully reviewed these websites to ensure that they are suitable for students. Many websites change frequently, however, and we cannot guarantee that a site's future contents will continue to meet our high standards of quality and educational value. Be advised that students should be closely supervised whenever they access the internet.

INDEX

Cascade Range, 16

Columbia River, 6, 7

Crater Lake National Park, 21

Deschutes National Forest, 8

Lewis and Clark National Park, 18

Mount Hood, 7

Mount St. Helens, 9

Native Americans, 12, 13

Newberry National Volcanic Monument, 8

Nez Perce National Historical Park, 13

North Cascades National Park, 18

Olympic National Forest, 7

Oregon, 4, 5, 7, 8, 14, 15, 16, 21

Oregon Dunes National Recreation Area, 17

Pacific Ocean, 5, 6

Puget Sound, 10, 11

Suquamish Museum, 13

volcano, 8

Washington, 4, 5, 7, 9, 11, 13, 14, 16, 21

weather, 4, 16, 17